# Memories in Poem and Song

## by

## R. E. Lyons

# In the U.S.A.

We're starving in the U.S.A

We're dying in the U.S.A

While Congress is Lying,

We all are dying,

Here in the U.S.A

# What a Day

What a day for a nightmare.<br>
A great big bundle of pain.<br>
What a day for a nightmare.<br>
With trouble to drive us insane.

We got a crazy congress,<br>
Who doesn't care about us at all.<br>
There just a bunch of millionaires.<br>
Who won't take care of our affairs.

They seem to think they own us.<br>
And want to see us die.<br>
They don't care about us.<br>
They only want to tell us lies.

No use of complaining<br>
We don't see eye to eye<br>
They're waiting for the corona virus<br>
To torment us till we die.

They sit and they judge us<br>
With money in their hands<br>
While we sit here starving<br>
All across this land.

Why we picked them to represent us<br>
I never will understand<br>
They vote laws to kill us<br>
They think they rule us grand

They think if they kill us<br>
The elderly, the disabled and poor<br>
We no longer will be a burden<br>
So they vote against us on the floor

They forget they can't do without us
Who else will do our jobs?
They won't dirty their hands
They're a rich bunch of snobs.

Who will pay our taxes?
So congress can pay the rich.
When it comes around to bite them
You know karma can be a bitch.

They will learn a lesson
But too late they will see
That they really need us
But dead we will be.

Fools have often have hindsight
But in front they cannot see
Congress is really foolish
They should be helping you and me.

The day will come when we will
Have a congress that really cares
But till then we will suffer
Now that isn't really fair.

So until then God keep you
Safe and out of their hands
Lord knows we need it
We don't really need their plans.

# Freedom

Dead soldier laying
On the battlefield
He fought for freedom
But his fate was sealed

He loved his family
With his heart and soul
He flew old glory proudly
On his flag pole

He was a good solder
A hell of a man
Who fought for his country?
With a gun in his hand

He will never be forgotten
For the brave things he done
I will say his name proudly
A true patriot son

I saw him fall slowly
Upon that bloody ground
His machine gun firing
Bringing our enemy down

He gave his all
With his last breath
He went down with honor
We will honor his death.

So when you see our flag flying
High there in the sky
Remember a fallen soldier
And remember why

Old glory is still waving

And a tear comes to your eye
It took soldier's love of country
Their willingness to die

To bring you your freedom
The peaceful blue sky
Because of his dying
And the blank look in his eye

## Luck of a Man

There is a beginning
There is an end
And in between
Is not what you intend

Though you try
As best you can
To make sense of it
To complete your plan

But try as you might
To get things done
To do it all
You have never won

For things happen
Out of your control
That rips your heart
Your very soul

Then all falls apart
Like dust in the wind
We all die alone
In the end.

But onward we try
To get what we can
Though we know we are defeated

That's the luck of a man

# No Longer a Man but Damned

Distance, Darkness, fade away,

Take me back to yesterday.

To a place before it began

Where I was not a beast, but a man.


Where the moon did not call to me,

Grab me, then transform me,

Changed to the beast that I am,

No longer a man, but damned.


How I long for yesterday,

Not a beast by night and man by day,

Oh how blessed it would be,

Oh how I long to be free.


All these human that would be saved,

If not their flesh and blood I craved,

Oh how I long for yesterday,

Where I never had to live this way.


**How I tire of this whining man,**

**His complaining is more than I can stand,**

Why can he not understand,

Thanks to me, he is free to roam this land.


For food he does not want,

He should be thankful to me what I hunt,

I give him freedom above the law,

I fear nothing while standing tall.


Hunger and thirst I never feel,

The fear of man is very real,

For I will take their life this very day,

Should they ever come my way.


You should be thankful for being me,

For together, you and I are we,

We need no clothing or coats to bear,

We keep warm with my long flowing hair.


But look at the lives that we destroy,

When we take life there can be no joy,

We feast upon our fellow man

The thought of it is more than I can stand.


If I could, I would Devour you too,

You irritate me for all the complaining you do,

Be careful now what you say,

Or I will not let you out even in the day.


You cannot do this, not even you,

May God save me from what you do,

But it's only the moon, that brings you out,

Of this I have no doubt.


You did not think it possible that I exist,

So this way of thinking, how can you insist?

Anything is possible, this you must agree

For if not that, how can I be?


You are a demon sent from Hell,

A most horrible curse that all men will tell

Of how you attacked them in the full moon light,

And the gruesome remains they find in the daylight.


It is only scraps of the food I eat,

You cannot expect me not to partake of the meat

It is so delicious and ever so sweet,

You must stop complaining of what you eat.

The very thought it sickens me

I beg of you be gone from me

Take yourself back to Hell itself

So I might have peace of mind and health.


**Ah the moon it rises so full and bright**

**It makes me stronger by its light**

**And finally it's silent this troublesome man**

**So I can be the killer of man.**

# Was the Night before Christmas

Was the night before Christmas
And all through the house
Not a creature was stirring
Not even a mouse


And though the ground was covered
from the new fallen snow
I was wishing it was morning
And the darkness would go


For I knew something was coming
I did not know when
But surely it was coming
And I didn't want it in


So there I was lying
All filled up with dread

*My body was sweating*
*from my toes to my head*

*For Christmas had no meaning*
*When I knew it would come*
*So I drank myself silly*
*till I was full of rum*

*I heard the clock ticking*
*I heard each loud stroke*
*My throat began tightening*
*Till I felt I would choke*

*But time had no ending*
*it kept dragging by*
*The room was so silent*
*I thought I would die*

*The danger was coming*
*I knew in my heart*
*Nothing could stop it*
*I wished it would part*

*Then came the vampire*
*In through the night*
*He bit my poor sister*
*what a horrible site*

*My sister was screaming*
*It was all she could do*
*for in a matter of seconds*
*her poor life was through.*
*I heard all the screaming.*
*and I quickly arose.*
*to find out what was the matter.*
*with my dear sister Rose*

*I got to my door.*
*I opened it wide.*
*then ran to her room.*
*to be by her side*

*He stood there smiling.*
*Mouth dripping with gore*
*my poor sister was lying.*
*with no blood on the floor*

*He saw me there standing.*

*not knowing what to do*

*he began to start laughing.*

*his feeding was through.*


*he tuned and he dashed.*

*for his freedom outside*

*he did not care who saw him.*

*he never tried to hide.*


*he was filled with such confidence.*

*he was filled with such pride.*

*I was filled with such loathing.*

*for my poor sister had died.*


*The full moon was rising.*

*it was shining so bright.*

*I began changing.*

*I was ready to fight.*


*The vampire was not ready.*

*for what happened that night*

*he was gleefully escaping.*
*he was full of delight.*


*he was happily running.*
*but suddenly stopped.*
*when he heard a beast growling*
*and felt the claws drop.*


*he felt his flesh ripping.*
*from the claws deep inside*
*for they cut him like butter*
*all the way down his dead hide*


*He stood there not moving.*
*his face showing surprise.*
*as the beast bit into him*
*you could see pain in his eyes.*


*For the beast he awakened*
*he should not you see.*
*for all he had done*
*brought the werewolf out in me.*

*I ate his dead flesh.*

*just out of spite*

*for his killing my sister*

*Well, it just wasn't right!*


*for all this dreading*

*I was feeling that night.*

*it was the werewolf's coming.*

*in the full moon light*

# Love Forever

Distance darkness seems the way

Though I Love you more every day


Sometimes there is misunderstanding

Sometimes there are obstacles with our planning


But through it all our love is strong

We stick together no matter what goes wrong


If this is not true love I don't know what is.

When we get through all the troubles there will be only bliss


We will be in each other's arms and kiss

No more will there be any time to miss.


We will hold each other in our arms

Protect each other from all harms


Be with each other night and day

Care for each other in a special way


All you need to do is believe in me my love

Thank the Lord for us being together from above


Believe with all your heart I will be there

For that moment on we will forever share


Our Love, Hope's and dreams as one

There together in the Filipino sun

# Winds of Time

Winds of time

Don't let the winds of time

Don't let the winds of time

Blow your mind away


First your born

Then you die

And in between

Well you just cry


When we were young

Everything was against us then

No matter how hard we tried

It seemed we would never win


But time kept moving on

We were ready face whatever came

Because we loved each other

You went and took my name


Winds of time

Don't let the winds of time

Don't let the winds of time

Blow your mind away


First your Born

Then you die

And in between

Well, you just cry


We had children together

We loved each and every one

We hoped the best for them all

Every daughter and son.


But fate was against us

We never had a chance

There was way too much coming

Though we tried with every circumstance


Winds of time

Don't let the winds of time

Don't let the winds of time

Blow your mind away


First you're born

Then you die

And in between

Well, you just cry


Now I am standing here

Now that your life is through

I am looking down on you

And I don't know what to do


We faced whatever came together

Now I am here all alone

And my heart is deeply broken

I don't know what to do


Winds of time

Don't let the winds of time

Don't let the winds of time

Blow your mind away.


First you're born

Then you die

And in between

Well, you just cry

Nothing can ever describe

How much you meant to me

I feel so totally lost

This not how it should be


But nothing has ever been

The way it should be

So why could I expect it now

For you or me.


Winds of time

Don't let the winds of time

Don't let the winds of time

Blow your mind away.


First your born

Then you die

And in between

Well, you just cry


Time wears down our spirits

The winds of time are constantly blowing

Trying to destroy everyone.

That we ever had going

Now I stand all alone

Time has taken you from me

All I have now are memories

And it's try to take that from me


Winds of time

Don't let the winds of time

Don't let the winds of time

Blow your mind away


First your born

Then you die

And in between

Well, you just cry


Winds of time

Winds of time


## I Want To Go To Heaven


I heard a crash on the highway

It was a cold and rainy day

And as he lay there dyeing

He began to pray


Oh Lord I want to go to heaven

I want to go up there

Oh Lord I want to go to heaven

I don't want to go down there


The fires of hell are burning

The devils waiting too

Oh Lord I want to go to heaven

I want to be with you


Up there the angels are singing

Their singing their praises to you

Oh Lord I want to go to heaven

I want to sing them too


From his eyes the tears were falling

I still remember today

The words that he was saying

The words that he did pray.


Oh Lord I want to go to heaven

I want to be up there

Oh Lord I want to go to heaven

I don't want to go down there


The fires of hell are burning

The devils waiting too

Oh Lord I want to go to heaven

I want to be with you


Up there the angels are singing

Their singing their praises to you

Oh Lord I want to go to heaven

I want to sing them too


Oh Lord I want to go to heaven

Please don't send me down there

# Tree of Woe

Tree of woe

Pass me by

Tree of woe

Don't make me cry


You have bent me down

On bended knee

You raked my soul

Made me see


All this sorrow

That will forever be

Burned it deep

In my memory


Tree of woe

Let me be

Tree of woe

Let me be


My heart is broken

It will never heal

My soul is weak

With this sorrow I feel


What must I do?

to make amends

How can I atone?

For these awful sins


Show mercy on me

And set me free

Tree of woe

Set me free


There is no forgiveness

For what I done

Wicked are the ways

Of this wicked one.


I have no excuses

There can be none

But still have mercy

On this wicked one.


Show me kindness

Please let me be

Tree of woe

Let me be

# When I Die

When I die
Will you cry?
Or shrug your shoulders
And not bat an eye

Would I have meant something to you?
Or simple be happy my life was though
Where I was no longer there
To be a burden to you

There is nothing in life that is clear
So few things that anyone holds dear
I simply don't know where I stand
Were you happy I was here

Though I tried my best
Seems I'm simply like all the rest
To you we are all the same
Someone to tolerate at best

So before I lay down my head
Before they pronounce me dead
I would truly like to know
Truly what you said.

Tell me what is truly in your heart
Before my death's journey start
How you really feel about me
Please speak from the heart

For this I truly want to know
For me I really love you so
But I want to hear from you
One last time before I go

When I die
Will you cry?

Or shrug your shoulders
And not bat an eye

# World in Utter Confusion

World in utter confusion
Trying to live in this illusion.

With everything trying to bring us down.
Trying to plant us in the ground.

There is not much we can turn too
When your true friends are only a few

So we hang by only a thread
Always fearing what we dread.

Hard to hang on with all of this
Remembering freedom we all miss

Hope you all are doing better than me
Cause I would never wish this on anyone you see.

I'm sure it will get better for all of you
God bless you in everything you do.

# I am not there, I did not die

Do not stand by my grave and weep.
I am not down there six feet deep

Do not cry out as you shed a tear
But instead hold memories of me oh so dear.

For I will always be with you here
I will be by your side ever so near

Watching over you and keep you
safe and sound in everything you do.

No, I did not die
Nor am I about to say goodbye

I have only shed this fleshly shell
I am not in heaven or hell

My time on this earth is not done.
My battles here are neither lost nor won.

It will only end on judgment day
When God decides yay or nay

So do not give up on me
For I am here where I was meant to be.

Standing here by your side
For I have not left nor have I died

I am here for eternity
So don't ever give up on me

Wipe those tears from your eye
You don't have to ever say goodbye.

# Life


In every life
A little rain must fall,
In every eye,
a tear must surely fall,

But through it all,
happy memories prevail,
As joy returns
While we relive a happy tale.

In every life there will always be
ups and downs,
It will be until at last,
They lower us into the ground.

Never surrendering
On this wild and crazy beast.
Or giving up
in the least.

Until we are shoved into
these worlds unknown.
While we scream proudly, I can take what is given
me on my own.

# To my brother Donnie

Rest my brother
Where there will be no pain
Rest my brother
where tears shall not remain

rest in the bosom of our people
of Days gone by
Safely In our mothers arms
where no more will you die

Rest my brother
No more trials must you face
Rest my brother
No more disappointments must you taste

where joy is there you will be
Don't worry brother
Soon you will turn and there I will be

# Four More Roses

By

James Rowland

R. E. Lyons


Four more roses

Four more roses

Laying there in momma's bed

Four More Roses

Laying there by momma's head


You know momma always loved the roses

And one day she said

You know son I've always loved the roses

And when I lay on my death bed

Please put 4 roses next to my head


Four more roses

For more roses

Laying there in momma's bed

Four more roses

Laying there by momma's head


Then one day

Momma fell to the floor

Her poor weak legs couldn't hold her anymore

And as I cared her to her bed

These are the last words my momma said

Four more roses

Four more roses

Laying there in momma's bed

Four more roses

Laying there by momma's head


And when I called the doctor

He came to check on her

He slowly shook his head

With sadness in his eyes

I'm sorry but your momma is dead.


Four more roses

Four more roses

Laying there in momma's bed

Four more roses

Your momma is dead.

# Won't You Help Me Sweet Jesus

Won't you help me sweet Jesus

For I'm really not that strong

Won't you help me Sweet Jesus?

For I don't know right from wrong


There is temptation tempting me lord

There is temptation tempting me

Won't you help me sweet Jesus

There is temptation tempting me


Won't you help me sweet Jesus

For I'm really not that strong

Won't you help me Sweet Jesus?

For I don't know right from wrong


There is trouble troubling me Lord

There is trouble troubling my soul

Won't you help me sweet Jesus

There is trouble troubling my soul


Won't you help me sweet Jesus

For I'm really not that strong

Won't you help me Sweet Jesus?

For I don't know right from wrong

# As I Sit In the Darkness

As I sit in the darkness

For a story to unfold

I listen for ancient stories

From those that never told


When time was fresh and new

Where treasure was treasured like gold

From people who have lived it

And had to be so bold


Where all life is a mystery

With fear at every turn

Where there is always something

That your heart will forever yearn


Where in the great unknown

There is always something to fear

Where courage fills us all

To protect the ones so dear


So is the life of a writer

To create these worlds and then

Be the greatest here

To fight the fight and win

Or lose a love so dear

That you will never go on

And end you life right here

For all hope is gone


Know one knows all the mysteries

That are unlocked within

Of a writers mind to tell

With a stroke of a pen


So if you care to read it

Buy my books and then

My stories will captivate you

From the beginning to the end

# Journey to Heaven

Travel on

To the great beyond

Though we cry

Now that your gone


But in the Lord

We put our trust

The Lord said come

So go you must


To be with you

In heaven above

Away from

All the ones you love


He took you there

To streets of gold

He gave to you

Your child to hold


He assured you that

In time they would come

To be with you

Don't let your heart go numb


So let peace

Come in your heart

for in truth

your never apart


You have to wait

only a little while

for soon they will come

it's only a trial


When we will greet them

At heaven's gate

All we have to do

Is sit and wait


Then all will be together

In my father's home

No one will be left behind

Out there to roam

Then here we will

Forever be

you and them

forever with me


With heavy hearts

They are now

but they will

Understand somehow


We are all together

That all is never lost

And will be forever

For this I paid the cost


This I give to you

To forever be

To be in paradise

For all to be with me

# My Love is Gone

My heart is aching

My Love your taking

My heart is breaking

My legs are shaking


All hope is gone

How can I go on?

See another dawn

With me all alone


Why did you do this to me?

I can't take this misery

How did this come to be?

I'm adrift on an endless sea


I sit and wonder why

All the time I sit and cry

I feel like I could simply die

Please Lord; tell me it's a lie


I feel like I'll go mad

These feeling that I had

It's hurting me so bad

It's much more than feeling sad


So what am I to do?

All my happiness is through

I feel so alone and blue

Because I want only you


But the Lord took you away

Not a word did I get to say

How can it end this way?

How can I even pray?


All this I hold inside

Not that I have any pride

It's not I haven't tried

I have nothing left to hide


I love only you

This much I know is true

I never said goodbye to you

Before your life was through


I no longer want to live

There is no more I can give

Why should I want to live?

My love to you I cannot give


I look at your body so cold

You were not given a chance to grow old

Jesus called you home I'm told

So why am I allowed to grow old?


I feel so useless now

I want to be with you somehow

But I'm lost to figure out how

Shall I follow you now?

I wrote this poem for a good friend of mine, about his loss. When I talked to him I found the church had added music to it. They will, I'm told, sing it every Sunday at bible school. They loved it so well. God bless them. Here are the lyrics


My Love is Gone By: R. E. LYONS
Music By: Louise Claire S. Moral
Dedicated To: Kuya Yhen, because he lost his beloved woman and son.


"My Love is Gone"
By
R. E. Lyons

My heart is aching
My Love your taking
My heart is breaking
My legs are shaking

All hope is gone
How can I go on?
See another dawn
With me all alone

CHORUS:
I love only you
This much I know is true
I never said goodbye to you
Before your life was through

Why did you do this to me?
I can't take this misery
How did this come to be?
I'm adrift on an endless sea

I feel like I'll go mad
These feeling that I had
It's hurting me so bad

It's more than feeling sad

So what am I to do?
All my happiness is through
I feel so alone and blue
Cause I want only you

(REPEAT CHORUS)
All this I hold inside
Not that I've any pride
It's not I haven't tried
I've nothing left to hide

I look at you so cold
You're not given a chance to grow old
Jesus called you home I'm told
So why am I allowed to grow

# When life has no meaning

When life has no meaning
Only sorrows to bear
When your left alone
With no one who cares?

When your accused
And all are lies
When you heart is broken
When tears floods your eyes

When your love is full of fantasies
Not one of them true
But shoves all of them
All down on you

When all the world
Is bringing you down
When all the weight
Pushes you to the ground

When you feel all forsaken
No one that really care
When there is nowhere to turn
Not one second of life is fare

What do you do?
When there's nothing for you
What really matters
When you feel life is through

Damn if I know
A thing I can do
I'm just as lost
As everyone of you

# I Come

I come in the darkness
When you least expect me
I come in the light
When you feel safe and free

I come to take
all I can from you
I come to destroy
Everything you do

I come to
Show you no mercy
I come to
Bring you agony

I come to
Bring you no good
I come to give you
All the pain that I could.

Yes I come. I come
For you cannot stop me
I come for nothing
Can ever stop me

I come for all you have gained
In this wicked old world
I come, I come
With my hands unfurled

Oh yes I come, I come
Though you beg me not too
I come, I come
And there is nothing you can do

I come for I

Am your destiny
I come because
I am your eternity

I come for you
Because it was what
I was created for
I come to keep you Forevermore

I come for
I am deaths decree
I come, I come
I come for thee

# People Say I'm Crazy

People say I'm crazy

They think I'm a fool

But I say they're crazy

They shouldn't be so cruel


always judging people

They ought to be ashamed

They're always causing heartache

But never the ones to blame


Someday they're gonna wake up

Someday they're gonna see

Someday they're gonna take up

All the blame they pushed on me


They think they can do things

They think no one can see

They think they can take up

Anything and be blame free


But the day is a comin

When they will get they're due

They'll be the ones a cryin

They're gonna be so blue


Someday they're gonna wake up

Someday they're gonna see

Someday they're gonna take up

All the blame they pushed on me


The time is a comin

Just you wait and see

They'll be begging for help

But they won't get it from me


Cause People say I'm crazy

They think I'm a fool

But I say they're crazy

They shouldn't be so cruel


Someday they're gonna wake up

Someday they're gonna see

Someday they're gonna take up

All the blame they pushed on me

Someday they're gonna take up

All the blame they pushed on me

# Regrets

There have been times
When I have been wrong
Times when I was weak
When I should have been strong

Times when I lashed out
To those that did no wrong
And never said a word
To those guilty all along

When the world gets all quiet I think of all these things
I could rip myself apart
For all the heartaches I bring
Do I regret All the bad things I done?

Yes i do
Every one
Can I change What has already past?
I'm doing my best To do good at last

They say it's hard
For an old man to change his ways
But he better be getting to it
For he don't have to many more days

And that saying is true
For we can't live forever
We need to learn to treat people right
And quit hurting people ever.

So forgive an old man
Who has seen the error of his ways
Who regrets ever hurting you
In this, the latter of my days

A man who has finally saw the light
Though it took a long time to do
I truly am sorry
For all the things wrong I done to you.

# All I'm Asking

I am standing right here
Waiting on you to love me
Waiting for the world to quit falling apart
Waiting on you to see

All I'm asking is to believe in me
All I'm asking is to believe in me
Everything will come together like it's suppose to be
All I'm asking is to believe in me

I know you had a hard life before
I know you don't want to have that anymore
I know I'm living on a distant shore
But one day I'll be there at your door

All I'm asking is to believe in me
All I'm asking is to believe in me
Everything will come together like it's suppose to be
All I'm asking is to believe in me

I'm knocking at your heart so let me in
Give me a chance to love you and then
So both our lives can start again
Only thing I need is to let me in

All I'm asking is to believe in me
All I'm asking is to believe in me
Everything will come together like it's suppose to be
All I'm asking is to believe in me

When we will be together so many years
You won't remember all those fears
You past won't bring you all those tears
Let me give you joy for many more years

All I'm asking is to believe in me
All I'm asking is to believe in me

Everything will come together like it's suppose to be
All I'm asking is to believe in me

All I'm asking to believe in me
All I'm asking is to believe in me
Take those tears away and set you free
All I'm asking is to believe on me